WORKING STEAM
Collett Granges & Manors

Ian Allan
PUBLISHING

Roy Hobbs

Introduction

With the production of the 'Hall' class well under way Chief Engineer C. B. Collett decided that the remaining '43xx' class 2-6-0s would require replacing. Their use on main-line passenger duties had been largely superseded by the 'Halls', and on freight workings by the '28xx' class 2-8-0s. With the heavier trains then becoming evident, it was decided to institute a rebuild programme; the earliest 43xx examples would be withdrawn for conversion into 4-6-0s. Wheels and motion would be retained and the Standard No 1 boiler, as fitted to the 'Halls', utilised. The first of this new 'Grange' class (68xx series), No 6800 *Arlington Grange,* was completed in August 1936 and entered service initially in the West Country, where its increased tractive effort, relative to the 'Halls', on the severe banks and curves of the Cornish main line proved a distinct advantage.

An additional factor was the better stability given by the leading bogie, which eliminated the well known 'nosing' characteristic of the 2-6-0s. With these improvements they quickly became favourites with loco crews, who often preferred them to the 'Halls', having regard to their improved acceleration.

Following this successful conversion it was decided that similar action would be needed in respect of those more minor lines where the Blue Route classification applied, equally restricting both 'Hall' and 'Grange' classes. Plans were accordingly made for the conversion of further '43xx' into a new design, the smaller 'Manor' (78xx series) class 4-6-0. Reconditioned wheels and motion would again be used, but this time a scaled-down No 1 Standard boiler would be employed. The first of 20 examples, No 7800 *Torquay Manor*, appeared in January 1938. Unfortunately a reputation for poor steaming was soon acquired, but it was not possible to seriously investigate this problem until after World War 2. Draughting modifications, in the blastpipe, chimney and grate areas following Swindon Test Plant experiments in the early 1950s made a radical improvement to the design, resulting in more than double the original power output being achieved.

A total of 80 'Granges' (Nos 6800-79) and 20 'Manors' (Nos 7800-19) had been completed by the outbreak of hostilities in 1939. Although the original plan had been to convert all the '43xx', the onset of the conflict plus Collett's retirement in 1941 halted this process. However, a further 10 'Manors' (Nos 7820-9), using new components, were completed in 1950.

Both designs were found extremely successful in their respective roles,

the 'Granges' being distributed widely across the system, and mainly used on fast freight and intermediate passenger duties. The 'Manors' like the 'Granges' were also widely spread, but came to be associated particularly with the Cambrian main line and piloting work in the West Country.

Withdrawals of both types started relatively slowly, No 6801 *Aylburton Grange* being the first casualty in October 1960, with only a further eight 'Granges' being despatched between 1961 and 1963. Of the 'Manors', only No 7809 *Childrey Manor* had disappeared by April 1963. However, with the rapid spread of dieselisation during 1964, some 26 'Granges' and some 10 'Manors' had gone by the year's end. No 6872 *Crawley Grange* and No 7829 *Ramsbury Manor* were recorded as the last members of their respective classes in service, both being withdrawn in December 1965.

As with previous volumes, information has come from a variety of sources, and I would particularly single out the *Great Western Railway Journal* (Wild Swan) and *Steam Days* (Redgauntlet) magazines in this respect, along with *Peto's Register of GWR Locomotives: Vol 2 Manor 4-6-0s* (Irwell Press). The usual loyal band of photographers have provided a comprehensive set of images for selection, and I am, once again, particularly indebted to them for their ongoing cooperation.

Roy Hobbs,
Exeter,
February 2003

First published 2003

ISBN 0 7110 2973 3

© Ian Allan Publishing Ltd 2003

Published by Ian Allan Publishing

an imprint of Ian Allan Publishing Ltd, Hersham, Surrey KT12 4RG.
Printed by Ian Allan Printing Ltd, Hersham, Surrey KT12 4RG.

Code: 0308/B1

Title page: In a not unusual role for one of the class 'Grange' No 6809 *Burghclere Grange* is shown piloting 'Modified Hall' class 4-6-0 No 7917 *North Aston Hall* through Sonning Cutting with an up express to Paddington on 3 May 1958. No 6809, built September 1936, had accumulated over 1 million miles in service before its withdrawal from Southall (81C) in July 1963. *T. B. Owen*

Below: One of the third series of Churchward-designed 2-6-0s No 6368, built 1925, is illustrated at Swindon on 26 March 1961. Though destined for similar rebuilding to either a 'Grange' or 'Manor' 4-6-0, as with the earlier '43xx' and '53xx' examples, this did not take place due to cancellation of the ongoing programme by F. W. Hawksworth when he assumed the position of Chief Engineer. *T. B. Owen*

Above: 'Grange' class prototype No 6800 *Arlington Grange* is illustrated here at Penzance (83G) MPD on 29 April 1961. Entering service in August 1936, its initial allocation was to this depot, followed by a period at Laira and then Landore. It returned to Penzance in October 1948 and, aside from a spell at Carmarthen (87G) around 1953, it stayed at the shed until transferred to Newport (86A), where it remained until withdrawal in June 1964. *R. C. Riley*

Right: Shortly after leaving Twyford, and on the approach to Sonning Cutting, No 6841 *Marlas Grange* heads a down semi-fast working on 5 December 1959. Around this time it was officially allocated to Bristol St Philips Marsh (82B), the depot then possessing one of the largest 'Grange' allocations, 17 being on strength and mainly used on a variety of goods duties. During the summer period a number found employment on the various cross-country holiday extras. *T. B. Owen*

Left: Frost remains evident on those sleepers shaded from the winter sun as No 6810 *Blakemere Grange* makes its way along the up relief line towards Twyford with a Class D freight, including a number of flat trucks holding mini-containers, on 27 January 1959. A small 3,500gal tender, of the type originally fitted to the 'Granges' is evident here, as compared with the larger 4,000gal version subsequently fitted to a large number of the class. *T. B. Owen*

Above: In the rather scruffy condition which appears to be a mark of the engines employed on these workings, No 6864 *Dymock Grange* heads towards Sonning with a down semi-fast service from Paddington on 21 April 1956. Along with No 6859 *Yiewsley Grange* it was allocated to Canton (86C) MPD in 1959 specifically to handle the banana traffic emanating from Barry Docks, although in practice working whatever duties were required at the time. *T. B. Owen*

Displaying the red reversing rod, a feature of locomotives repaired at the Caerphilly Works of the former Rhymney Railway, No 6828 *Trellech Grange,* still well prepared externally, heads along the up relief line towards Twyford on 19 April 1958 with a Class D mixed freight consisting mainly of van traffic. One of only five engines withdrawn in 1963, it worked like many others from Oxley (84B) MPD towards the close of steam operation. This depot, latterly under LMR control and re-coded 2B, had the largest number of the class during early 1963 when 16 were allocated to cover 12 freight diagrams. A considerable number of these duties involved interchange traffic to and from Crewe throughout the week.
T. B. Owen

With the North Downs featuring as a backdrop, No 7818 *Granville Manor* of Tyseley (84E) MPD departs Betchworth station on the SR cross-country route from Redhill to Reading with the 4.04pm local service from Redhill in September 1963. During November 1963 it worked throughout on the daily Banbury to Redhill goods trip, a most unusual duty for the class. *Roy Hobbs*

Left: Illustrated in charge of a return holiday train from the south coast, the 12.20pm Hastings–Birmingham Snow Hill via Redhill and Oxford, No 7805 *Broome Manor* is shown with its train of SR stock heading towards Buckland Crossing, east of Betchworth, on 31 August 1963. These through workings had started to decline from around 1960 and had further diminished by the following summer. *Roy Hobbs*

Above: Seen shortly after leaving Reigate station with the 11.35am Redhill–Reading local service, No 7816 *Frilsham Manor* takes the downhill stretch towards Betchworth in January 1964. It is attached to the well-known tender still bearing the final style 'GWR' lettering. Some two to three years earlier, this had been coupled to '43xx' class 2-6-0 No 6324 and, on transfer, remained with No 7816 until its withdrawal from Gloucester (85B) in November 1965. *Roy Hobbs*

Below: From August 1964 Didcot (81E) MPD continued to provide an engine for the daily WR duty over the Reading–Redhill route, until line dieselisation occurred in January 1965. No 7829 *Ramsbury Manor* had the doubtful honour of hauling the final working, the 11.35am from Redhill on 2 January 1965. It is depicted here on a snowy December day during 1964, slowly moving off Redhill MPD to take up its return trip. *Roy Hobbs*

Right: On a bright spring morning in May 1963, No 7813 *Freshford Manor* removes the ECS of the 6.50am Reading–Redhill away from Redhill station. This regular working was probably to maintain WR crew familiarity with the route, in view of the seasonal through passenger operations undertaken by them. Throughout the 1950s and up to around 1961/2 these duties were predominantly in the care of the '43xx' class 2-6-0s. *Roy Hobbs*

Left: Seen on the approach to Yeovil (Pen Mill), close to Yeovil South Junction 'box, which judging by the signal aspects has been switched out, No 6821 *Leaton Grange* heads northward with a van train from Weymouth on 18 July 1964. This was the first of its class, in May 1954, to be fitted with the AK pattern boiler employing a three-row superheater. All remaining class members were dealt with subsequently. These boilers were interchangeable with those on the 'Hall' class and replaced indiscriminately. *P. W. Gray*

Above: A view at Weymouth (71G) MPD, now in SR territory, of an ex-works engine, on this occasion No 7814 *Fringford Manor*. Seen on 18 May 1962, it had undergone a Heavy Intermediate inspection at Swindon and was probably on a running-in turn. It spent the following two years or so in West Wales, where it would often be seen working the Aberystwyth–Carmarthen services. Transferred in September 1963 from Carmarthen (87G) to Llanelly (87F), it was condemned at Gloucester (85B) in September 1965. *C. L. Caddy*

Above: Shortly after leaving Whiteball Tunnel, No 6814 *Enborne Grange* starts its descent of Wellington Bank with the 10.40am Paignton–Derby (duty M21) on 9 June 1962. The two-mile downhill run is, of course, associated with the 1904 record of 'City' class 4-4-0 *City of Truro*. No 6814 was another of those class members likely to have exceeded a million miles in service prior to its December 1963 withdrawal. *P. W. Gray*

Right: On a beautifully clear summer evening No 6827 *Llanfrecha Grange* heads past Exeter West box and across the River Exe with the 3.55pm Pylle Hill–Newton Abbot parcels duty on 23 June 1962. Approaching is 'Modified Hall' No 7909 *Heveningham Hall* with a return excursion from Goodrington to the SR. The steeply graded Southern line via Exeter Central to Waterloo disappears to the left of the picture. *R. C. Riley*

Left: Alongside the River Exe estuary, No 6834 *Dummer Grange* passes through Starcross with the 2.15pm Plymouth–Cardiff on 28 June 1959. The tower in the background belongs to one of the pumping stations used in connection with Brunel's abortive atmospheric railway of the 1840s. *P. W. Gray*

Below: No 6811 *Cranbourne Grange* heads an up ECS working by the sea wall between Teignmouth and Dawlish on 14 July 1958. This locomotive became the first 'Grange' to be paired with a Collett 3,500gal tender, later replaced, in August 1944. *R. C. Riley*

Left: No 7809 *Childrey Manor* heads the 5.37pm Newton Abbot–Kingswear service near Aller Junction, on 18 July 1958. The first of the class to be condemned, it was withdrawn from Shrewsbury (89A) MPD in April 1963. The 'Manors' appeared in the West Country from 1948 onwards to assist the 'Halls' and 'Granges' on piloting duties, and to hasten the withdrawal of the elderly 'Bulldog' 4-4-0s still employed on this work. For these reasons six were allocated to the Newton Abbot Division. *R. C. Riley*

Above: Seen alongside the River Dart estuary between Paignton and Kingswear, No 6874 *Haughton Grange* has charge of a down local service on 18 July 1958. Following a freight train derailment at Sampford Peverell in March 1954, No 6874 was found working a down freight duty amongst other WR locomotive types diverted over the SR main line from Yeovil to Exeter. Trials over this route in the spring of 1953 had originally declared the class 'out of gauge'! *T. B. Owen*

Getting to grips with Dainton Bank, shortly after passing Aller Junction, No 6802 *Bampton Grange* is seen with the 9.05am Swansea–Penzance service on 3 July 1957. It was the third member of the class to be withdrawn, in August 1961. Along with No 6805 *Broughton Grange* it became one of the only two examples to disappear that year. Back in the early 1950s it had been allocated to Laira (83A) MPD, where, a typical Saturday duty could have been diagram LA46: 6.28am passenger Plymouth to Newquay (originating as the 9.15pm (Friday) ex-Manchester), the 11.00am Newquay (for York) to Plymouth, followed by 2.08pm (pilot) Plymouth to Newton Abbot with the 11.00am Penzance–Wolverhampton. *R. C. Riley*

In a further view of the climb to Dainton Summit No 6809 *Burghclere Grange* pilots 'Castle' class 4-6-0 No 5082 *Swordfish* with the first portion of the down 'Cornish Riviera Express' on 20 April 1962, this being Good Friday. A Penzance (83G) resident through much of the 1950s, No 6809 was based at Bristol St Philips Marsh (82B) in the early 1960s before final allocation to Southall (81C) in October 1962. *P. W. Gray*

Below: Having surmounted Dainton Bank No 6842 *Nunhold Grange* passes Dainton Tunnel 'box with a short Class C van working on 19 June 1958. It was one of a number of the class that spent many years allocated to a single depot, being based at Bristol St Philips Marsh (82B) from build in September 1937 to January 1962, when transfer to Penzance (83G) took place. *T. B. Owen*

Right: Heading eastwards towards the tunnel entrance, No 6855 *Saighton Grange* passes Dainton Tunnel 'box with an eight-coach up local service on 18 July 1958. A Newton Abbot Division engine at this time, it operated in the Wolverhampton Division during the 1960s, being based mainly at Oxley (84B) MPD; it also worked from Tyseley (84E), where withdrawal occurred in October 1965. *T. B. Owen*

ALL DOWN
Goods and Mineral Trains
WITH 35 WAGONS OR LESS
MUST STOP DEAD HERE

6855

ALL DOWN
Goods and Mineral Trains
with 35 Wagons or Less
Must STOP DEAD here

Left: A further view in the vicinity of Dainton Tunnel, with No 6860 *Aberporth Grange* double-heading 'Hall' class 4-6-0 No 5999 *Wollaton Hall*, itself withdrawn in September 1962. The train is the 7.50am Newquay–Manchester and was photographed on 12 August 1961. No 6860 moved around various divisions throughout its working life from February 1939 until February 1965, but during the late 1950s was operating mainly in the West Country. However, with the dieselisation of most services in this region, condemnation eventually came at Cardiff East Dock (88A) MPD. *P. W. Gray*

Right: No 6845 *Paviland Grange* pilots 'Hall' class 4-6-0 No 6913 *Levens Hall* west of Dainton Summit with the 7.55am Camborne–Bristol relief working on 31 July 1959. Built in October 1937 it was eventually withdrawn in September 1964 from Tyseley (2A) depot. One quoted event concerning No 6845 was reported by WR fireman Dick Potts, as follows:

'On one trip on which I was firing, we came down towards Leamington at such a pace that vibration ceased and we seemed to be floating — a most peculiar feeling! An enthusiast friend who timed our train recorded a speed of 90mph past Fosse Road 'box, telling the guard that we were really "having a go"! We eventually made up 25 minutes of a late departure from Swindon'. *P. W. Gray*

Above: During dieselisation, steam power was often used in tandem with the new traction. Here No 6849 *Walton Grange* pilots 'Warship' class No D824 *Highflyer* at Tigley on the 10.40am (Sun) Paddington–Newquay/Falmouth service on 11 September 1960. No 4947 *Nanhoran Hall* passes on the 2.15pm Plymouth-Cardiff. *P. W. Gray*

Right: No 6837 *Forthampton Grange* is shown piloting a further example of modern traction, No D817 *Foxhound*, in charge of an unidentified holiday train, near Brent, in September 1960. Following a spell at Penzance (83G) MPD during the 1950s, No 6837 moved to Llanelly (87F) in the 1960s. *K. W. Wightman*

Below: No 6832 *Brockton Grange* leads '47xx' class 2-8-0 No 4705 on the steep gradients of Hemerdon Bank with the 10.00am (SO) Newquay–Paddington, on 14 June 1958. Back in January 1948 No 6832 took over the 12.20pm Cardiff–London at Swindon from a failed 'Britannia' Pacific and proceeded to record a net time of 80 minutes for the remaining 77 miles to Paddington, a remarkable feat for this small-wheeled locomotive. *T. B. Owen*

Right: No 7809 *Childrey Manor* pilots 'King' class 4-6-0 No 6013 *King Henry VIII* up Hemerdon with a Perranporth–Paddington working on 14 June 1958. No 7809's final depot was Shrewsbury (then 6D) which during 1963 was responsible for four 'Manor' diagrams, comprising one passenger and three freight. These included the 'Cambrian Coast Express' both ways on Saturdays, plus the Aberystwyth–Crewe mails duty. *T. B. Owen*

Above: Standing alongside the coaling plant at Plymouth Laira (83D) MPD on 15 July 1956, No 7823 *Hook Norton Manor,* had recently returned to the Newton Abbot Division following a brief allocation to Neath (87A). It is shown in the plain black livery probably applied at its Heavy General overhaul the previous March. This scheme applied from 1953 until July 1956, when lined green was applied progressively to the whole class. *R. C. Riley*

Right: Heading through the Plymouth suburbs on 2 March 1963 with the 3.00pm Plymouth–Cardiff, No 6808 *Beenham Grange* is tackling the climb towards Mutley Tunnel. A Penzance (83G) engine throughout the 1950s and into the 1960s, it was transferred to Cardiff East Dock (88L) prior to withdrawal from Oxley (2B) in August 1964. Over a million miles were recorded before the keeping of these details ceased at the close of 1963. *T. W. Nicholls*

A view featuring both classes covered in this album shows No 7813 *Freshford Manor* piloting No 6832 *Brockton Grange* over St Pinnock Viaduct, the tallest on the Cornish main line, between Bodmin Road and Doublebois with the 10.00am Newquay–Paddington on 13 September 1958. No 7813 is coupled to one of Collett's 'Intermediate' 3,500gal tenders, here No 2377, 10 of which were constructed in 1925/6. Six of these ran at times with 10 different 'Manors'. Higher than those of Churchward's design, they also incorporated full-length fenders. *T. B. Owen*

Heading down the Cornish main line No 6800 *Arlington Grange* pilots 'Hall' class 4-6-0 No 6941 *Fillongley Hall* across Clinnick Viaduct on 8 August 1959, with a further working of the 10.00am Newquay– Paddington. During the 1950s Penzance (83G) and Bristol St Philips Marsh (82B) had the largest allocations of 'Granges', between 10 and 12 being based at each depot. *P. W. Gray*

Below: No 6805 *Broughton Grange* leaves Truro station with a down freight on 15 May 1959. Postwar allocations included Cardiff (Canton) (then CDF), Bristol St Philips Marsh (82B) and finally Newport (86A). It was an early withdrawal being taken out of service in March 1961; No 6802 *Bampton Grange* was the only other 'Grange' condemned that year, in August. *M. Mensing*

Right: Presumably having just left Truro depot, No 6826 *Nannerth Grange* heads towards the main line before taking up its next duty on 8 April 1960. Considered by Penzance (83G) to be its best engine, No 6826 is noteworthy as having achieved the greatest mileage within the class, a figure of 1,072,575 having been recorded at the close of 1963. The average for the class was around 904,000. *R. C. Riley*

Left: Close to Penwithers Junction, west of Truro, No 6863 *Dolhywel Grange*, in apparent ex-works condition, leaves Higher Town Tunnel with the 10.18am Paddington–Penzance parcels working on 28 April 1962. The photographer discovered this unexpected bonus whilst returning from a railtour on the Newham goods branch as, when he was about to join the road above the tunnel, No 6863 suddenly appeared from its mouth! *P. W. Gray*

Above: No 6873 *Caradoc Grange* approaches Chacewater Summit with a Paddington–Penzance relief working on 16 May 1959. Authority O. S. Nock has quoted a run during the period with this engine coupled to a 'Hall' class 4-6-0, taking over the down 'Cornish Riviera' at Newton Abbot. On the severe climb to St Austell, speed was no lower than 26½ mph, and but for a check before Truro, 10 minutes would have been gained on schedule. *M. Mensing*

No 6818 *Hardwick Grange* at Swindon following completion of a heavy overhaul on 1 April 1959. Whilst hauling an Avonmouth–Salisbury freight in February 1947 the locomotive was mistakenly diverted over the Pilning single line at Hallen Marsh Junction, and a violent collision followed with a Cardiff-Avonmouth working hauled by a tender-first '90xx' 4-4-0. Both engines along with their tenders and some 26 wagons, were derailed, all sustaining considerable damage with several wagons being written off. *T. B. Owen*

No 6831 *Bearley Grange* stands in Swindon Works yard on 23 July 1961. Unlike No 6818 it is paired with a larger Collett 4,000 gal tender, first introduced on the class in 1942 when 24 engines were so fitted. Each of the class received one of these tenders for varying periods during their working lives between 1942 and 1960. Seventeen Collett 3,500gal tenders, as illustrated opposite, were also attached to most class members within their lifetimes. *T. B. Owen*

Below: No 6803 *Bucklebury Grange* is seen approaching Bristol Temple Meads with a lengthy van train on 14 November 1963. Throughout the 1950s it had been based at Stourbridge (84F) MPD, where a typical duty could have been the 12.45am Stourbridge–Llanelly (9.50pm ex-Bordesley) and 9.15pm Llandilo Junction–Stourbridge, this alternating with a Llanelly (87F) engine. *T. W. Nicholls*

Right: When this photograph was taken, on 10 March 1965, most of the 'Granges' had lost their nameplates and several their cabside numberplates. Fortunately No 6848, originally *Toddington Grange*, still retained the latter when photographed passing Bristol East 'box with what appears to be a ballast working. Withdrawal came at Worcester (85A) MPD in 1965. *T .W. Nicholls*

42

In this unusual view taken from the Severn Bridge on 20 June 1964, No 6811 *Cranbourne Grange* heads a southbound departmental working on the line between Gloucester and Chepstow. No 6811 was observed as late as March 1964 working the Fawley (SR)–Bromford Bridge oil tank train, at one time a frequent duty for one of these engines. By this time the working had been diagrammed for a BRCW Type 3 (D65xx) diesel, which was obviously unavailable on this occasion. Constructed in November 1936, No 6811 was withdrawn in July 1964, shortly after these workings, from Oxley (2B) MPD, the final home for so many of the class. *T. B. Owen*

Undy water troughs is the location for this view of No 6858 *Woolston Grange* on an up passenger duty on 4 August 1962. Whilst working the 8.55am Bournemouth–Leeds on 15 August 1964, this locomotive was incorrectly taken forward to Sheffield (Victoria), where platform coping was dislodged! Due to the lack of a replacement engine, it then continued via Denby Dale to Huddersfield, driven by an ER locomotive inspector, immaculately attired in blue pinstripe suit and Homburg hat! It returned 'out of gauge' to Oxley some 10 days later *J. Wiltshire*

Descending Llanvihangel Bank, near Abergavenny, with a Class E freight consisting mainly of 16-ton mineral wagons, No 6872 *Crawley Grange* was photographed on 1 April 1964 against the backdrop of the 1,200ft high Coalpit Hill. Llanvihangel Bank presented a considerable obstacle to trains in the opposite direction, freight workings often requiring banking assistance. A Pontypool Road (86G) engine throughout the 1950s, until transfer to Severn Tunnel Junction (86E) in 1964, No 6872 would have seen regular use on this line. One 1950s diagram involved the 10.35am to Saltney, returning with the 9.00pm to Harlescott, both being Class E workings. *Martin Smith*

On the picturesque route between Hereford and Gloucester, No 7814 *Fringford Manor* crosses the River Wye, near Backney, with a three-coach local working to Gloucester on 3 October 1964. This was a regular route for these engines from June 1964 until line closure, which took effect on 2 November 1964. Apart from this duty, Gloucester (85B) had diagrams which included the 5.20pm Weymouth-Bristol, the 12.45pm (SO) Gloucester–Swindon passenger and local goods trips. *Martin Smith*

Above: No 6836 *Estevarney Grange* is seen in charge of
a down Class F freight, near St Mellons, on 1 June 1963. It was
withdrawn from Worcester (85A) in August 1965, the depot having
two 'Grange' duties at this period with trips to Paddington and
Oxford, plus a Margam–Kidderminster working. *A. A. Jarvis*

Right: No 7805 *Broome Manor* leaves Pengam Junction coal yard on
8 June 1963. It was originally transferred to Cardiff in 1958, along
with three other 'Manors', to replace '43xx' class 2-6-0s on local
stopping services. No 7805 was notable in being one of only two
'Manors' to visit Caerphilly Works for repairs. *A. A. Jarvis*

Left: Seen at Newtown on 24 August 1963, No 6847 *Tidmarsh Grange* makes its way back to Cardiff East Dock (88L) MPD. Constructed in October 1937, it spent the first years following nationalisation in the Wolverhampton Division, but through the greater part of the 1950s was allocated to Newport (86A) depot. Following this it was transferred first to Canton (86C) and then Cardiff East Dock prior to ending its days at Worcester (85A) before condemnation in December 1965. *J. Wiltshire*

Above: In a further view taken east of Cardiff, from Newtown West signalbox, No 6813 *Eastbury Grange* heads towards the city with an ECS working. No 6813 was amongst the last six engines of the class to receive a Heavy General overhaul at Swindon, this taking place at the close of 1963. It was a resident of Newton Abbot (83A) depot throughout the 1950s, before transfer to Newport (Ebbw Junction) (86A) in the 1960s and final withdrawal from Worcester (85A) in September 1965. *A. A. Jarvis*

Seen with wagons receiving locomotive ash for disposal, No 6867 *Peterston Grange* stands alongside the coaling plant at Cardiff East Dock depot on 16 September 1962. For at least 10 years from around 1948 No 6867 was based at Bristol St Philips Marsh (82B) depot. Goods duties during this period involved turns to the West Country, Weymouth and along the North & West route to Shrewsbury and Chester, plus occasional passenger work. Subsequent allocations included Pontypool Road (86G) and Llanelly (87F). Final withdrawal took place from this latter depot in August 1964. *A.A. Jarvis*

A last swansong for the 'Grange' class was the working of the RCTS/SLS joint railtour of west Wales on 26 September 1965, when No 6859 *Yiewsley Grange* hauled the six-coach special on a return trip to Fishguard Harbour. The train is shown awaiting departure from Swansea High Street. Back in December 1952, whilst climbing Gresford Bank with a Birkenhead to London freight, this locomotive had been involved in a tragic incident. As the result of a faulty water-gauge reading the firebox crown collapsed, causing severe injuries to the fireman, the driver suffering severe shock. *T. J. Edgington*

The Carmarthen–Aberystwyth route was a particular haunt of the 'Manors' in later years. Here an extremely careworn No 7826 *Longworth Manor* heads across the River Towy at Carmarthen with the 5.50pm working to Aberystwyth on 6 August 1963. For some unexplained reason this locomotive seems to have been the least-photographed member of the class. A Carmarthen (87G) engine from 1953 to 1963, it probably spent the greater part of its operational life on the rather isolated Aberystwyth route, involving both passenger and freight duties. It continued working this line up to its closure in February 1965 and was withdrawn in April 1965. *Martin Smith*

Seen with a through working to Fishguard, No 7829 *Ramsbury Manor* departs Johnston, junction for Milford Haven, on 25 March 1963. Like No 7826 pictured opposite, it was a Carmarthen (87G) engine for much of its life before transferring to Llanelly (87F) in April 1964, and is known to have worked the 'Pembroke Coast Express' during this time. Withdrawal came from Gloucester (85B) in December 1965 following periods at Reading (81D) in May 1964 and Didcot (81E) from the following October. *A. A. Jarvis*

Left: The winter of 1962/3 was notorious as the most lengthy and severe since that of 1946/7. In this spectacular view, taken at West Ealing on 12 January 1963, No 6869 *Resolven Grange* is seen battling along the up relief line with a lengthy mixed freight. Underlining the severe nature of the prevailing conditions, the photographer quoted the maximum temperature as being in the region of -5°C! No 6869 was withdrawn from Cardiff East Dock (then 88A) in July 1965. *Martin Smith*

Above: No 6833 *Calcot Grange* approaches Aynho Junction with the 9.42am Bournemouth–Birkenhead summer working on 7 July 1962. The train is composed of SR stock, the respective regions concerned each providing sets for these long through duties. No 6833 had originally worked outward with the 8.43am Wolverhampton–Portsmouth Harbour, and a change to SR motive power would have probably occurred at Oxford. This was a regular weekend task for class members normally employed on freight work. *T. B. Owen*

Above: Banbury station is the location for this view of No 7824 *Iford Manor* heading south, with what is probably the 10.35am (SO) Birmingham–Hastings, on 28 July 1962. In 1961/2 this locomotive was a resident of Stourbridge depot (84F) and its passenger operations were usually confined to the Wolverhampton–Dudley–Worcester services, goods work being foremost. *T. W. Nicholls*

Right: The last of the 'Grange' class No 6879 *Overton Grange,* built in 1939, is seen at Banbury (then 2D) MPD on 12 October 1963. Based at Tyseley (84E) it could have worked to Banbury on the 5.12am goods from Washwood Heath; this continued forward as the 9.40am to Old Oak Common, returning next day with the 5.55am to Bordesley Junction. *R. C. Riley*

Banbury once again with a passably clean No 6825 *Llanvair Grange* heading an up local towards Reading in May 1963. As mentioned earlier, each 'Grange' was attached initially to a Churchward 3,500gal tender originating from either a '43xx' class 2-6-0 or '28xx' class 2-8-0. No 6825 was the first of 24 to be paired, in 1942, with the Collett 4,000gal version. The smaller tender actually took an extra ton of coal which was useful for long-distance freight work. No 6825 was also one of a number which spent several years at one depot; in this case Penzance (83G) where it remained from April 1940 until September 1960. With area dieselisation, it was transferred from St Blazey (83E) to Reading (81D) in October 1962. Withdrawal followed from Bristol St Philips Marsh (82B) in June 1964. *T. J. Edgington*

Approaching the summit of Hatton Bank, No 6871 *Bourton Grange* heads what is probably the 1.11pm Portsmouth Harbour–Wolverhampton on 8 August 1964. This locomotive was the last of its class to undergo a Heavy Casual repair at Swindon, between March and July 1964. Transferred to Oxley (84B) during 1960, it was withdrawn from that depot in October 1965. *M. Mensing*

Left: Against a background of local industry, No 6858 *Woolston Grange* edges away from Stratford-upon-Avon with a Class H working in the Honeybourne direction during 1961. The engine is particularly presentable, suggesting a recent visit to Swindon for attention. The small tender is also noteworthy. It was another example from the final six to receive a Heavy General overhaul, entering Swindon in October 1963. Withdrawal came at Tyseley (84E) in October 1965. *D. Penney*

Above: Along the section of line between Honeybourne and Cheltenham, which today forms part of the Gloucestershire Warwickshire Railway route between Toddington and Cheltenham Racecourse, No 7815 *Fritwell Manor* heads the 3.55pm Leamington Spa–Gloucester via Stratford-upon-Avon, having passed the closed station of Winchcombe on 22 August 1964. The working was unusual, normally being covered by a DMU at this time. *M. Mensing*

A down ECS working from Tyseley carriage sidings heads through Small Heath & Sparkbrook towards Birmingham Snow Hill on 7 May 1960. The train is made up of suburban stock that will eventually form the basis of two departures during the evening rush hour. A rather scruffy No 6856 *Stowe Grange* is in charge of this duty. Constructed in November 1937, it was a Wolverhampton (Stafford Road) (84A) engine early in the BR era, being transferred in the mid-1950s to Worcester (85A), where it remained until withdrawal in November 1965. By 1963 the latter depot had two 'Grange' freight diagrams. One three-day cycle, WOS401, covered the 10.00pm Worcester to Paddington (MWF), the 11.30pm Paddington-Worcester (TTh), or 'as ordered' Paddington–Oxford (SO) and the 3.45am (Sun) Oxford–Worcester. *M. Mensing*

Passing Birmingham Moor Street and approaching Snow Hill tunnel with a freight duty is No 6855 *Saighton Grange*, previously illustrated in Devon on passenger work. Whilst at Tyseley (84E), from where it was withdrawn in October 1965, it covered freight turns to Banbury, Evesham and Old Oak Common, often on a two- or three-day cycle. *M. Mensing*

Below: No 6866 *Morfa Grange* enters Birmingham Snow Hill with a short Class K mixed freight on 16 December 1961. This locomotive was notable in being allocated to Tyseley (84E) for its whole career, from construction in March 1939 until withdrawal in May 1965. Amongst other duties, Tyseley's engines acted as pilots at Birmingham Snow Hill, when required. *M. Mensing*

Right: No 6861 *Crynant Grange* is seen heading through Oakengates, near Wellington (Salop), with a Class C freight on 18 August 1962. The presence of two cattle wagons with occupants will be noted! No 6861 was another of the last six engines to undergo a Heavy General inspection, being admitted to Swindon during October 1963. *T. B. Owen*

Left: Seen near Carno in August 1965 with the down 'Cambrian Coast Express' No 7804 *Baydon Manor* is bereft of much identification but has its number crudely chalked on the smokebox door. By this time the remaining 'Manors' were generally in a very unkempt state, and were no longer the main source of motive power on the Cambrian lines. BR Standard Class 4MT 4-6-0s had largely taken over this particular duty, the remaining services being dieselised. *Roy Hobbs*

Above: Forging its way up the final stage of the 1-in-52 gradient of the Talerddig incline on the Cambrian main line between Machynlleth and Moat Lane Junction, No 7821 *Ditcheat Manor* heads the 10.45am Aberystwyth–Manchester on 8 August 1964. This is one of the eight 'Manors' rescued from Barry scrapyard, being removed in June 1981. Subsequently overhauled, it is currently on loan to the Great Central Railway at Loughborough. *P.W. Gray*

A further view of the last of the 'Manor' class, No 7829 *Ramsbury Manor,* as it tackles the over two miles Talerddig gradient above Llanbrynmair with the 9.55am Aberystwyth–Shrewsbury train on 19 April 1954. Predominantly a Carmarthen (87G) engine throughout the 1950s it was employed chiefly on the line to Aberystwyth. Typical workings would have been the 7.10am (MWF) or 9.00am (MWF) pick-up goods to Aberystwyth, returning with the 8.05am (TThS) or 10.30am (TThS) balancing turns. On alternate days these workings were mainly in charge of Aberystwyth's '43xx' class 2-6-0s. Other local passenger and goods duties were also covered, these embracing the Neyland and Pembroke Dock portions of expresses including the 'Pembroke Coast Express'. *T. B. Owen*

The four locomotives selected for use on the Royal Tour of Wales which took place in August 1963 are seen being prepared for this duty at Machynlleth (89C) depot. From right to left are Nos 7822 *Foxcote Manor*, 7819 *Hinton Manor*, 7828 *Odney Manor* and 7827 *Lydham Manor*. By one of those serendipitous events they are all still in existence, having been consigned to the Barry scrapyard on withdrawal, and now operate on various private lines in the Midlands, Wales and the Southwest. *D. Penney*

Left: Crew members of No 7827 *Lydham Manor* and No 7828 *Odney Manor* proudly pose with their charges as they wait for the Royal Party at Aberdovey on 9 August 1963. The ECS had been brought to this point for the commencement of their Welsh tour. Both locos were officially standby engines. Today No 7827 is based on the Paignton & Dartmouth Railway and No 7828 on the West Somerset Railway. *D. Penney*

Above: Rounding the curve at Dovey Junction with a lengthy train, No 7810 *Draycott Manor* is seen bearing the 'stopping train' headcode as it heads in the Aberystwyth direction on 3 June 1963. Transfer to Oswestry (89A) depot had taken place in 1959, by which time the shed had eight 'Manors' covering seven diagrams, comprising two passenger, four goods and one 'special'. One was a trip to Crewe, starting with the 12.35pm ex-Aberystwyth and returning on the 7.45pm Crewe–Whitchurch. *T. J. Edgington*

Below: No 7800 *Torquay Manor* departs Borth with a coast-line local on 23 May 1962. Built in January 1938, it was based at Banbury until transferred to Tyseley (84E) in June 1949. This first allocation was to enable it to take over, at Banbury, the Newcastle–Swansea through train, replacing a '43xx' 2-6-0. This was known unofficially as the 'Ports-to-Ports Express'. *J. G. Dewing*

Right: Recalling an earlier era and in splendid external condition when photographed near Bow Street on 16 May 1959, No 7811 *Dunley Manor* heads a through working to Paddington comprising a rake of coaches in the chocolate-and-cream livery of the old company. A further engine allocated to Banbury in 1938 for the Newcastle–Swansea trains, No 7811 would be withdrawn at Cardiff East Dock (then 88A) in July 1965. *T. B. Owen*

Left: Passing the locomotive shed, No 7801 *Anthony Manor* sets off from Aberystwyth with a main-line working to Shrewsbury on 22 December 1958. In 1949, when based at Laira, it appeared with the up 'Cornish Riviera Express' on an 'exchange' duty along the SR route via Okehampton, being piloted by SR 'T9' class 4-4-0 No 30716! It was also involved, along with No 7806 *Cockington Manor,* on Royal Train duties on 2/3 July 1952, in connection with the Newton Abbot Show, taking the stock through to Thorverton for overnight stabling.
T. B. Owen

Above: In this photograph, taken along the former Cambrian main line between Whitchurch and Welshpool, No 7819 *Hinton Manor* is seen passing the tiny Arddleen Halt with an Oswestry-Welshpool local service in November 1964. As mentioned previously, this locomotive is preserved along with eight other 'Manors', and currently based on the Severn Valley Railway at Bridgnorth. Having returned to service there in late 1977, it has since been used on a variety of main-line excursions and featured prominently in the 1985 'GW150' celebrations.
Roy Hobbs

It is fortunate that so many of the 'Manor' class survived long enough at Barry to be taken into the care of the growing preservation movement, being eminently suited for the various former GWR branch lines now in private hands. Restored No 7808 *Cookham Manor*, privately purchased from BR at the close of steam operation, pilots 'Hall' class 4-6-0 No 6998 *Burton Agnes Hall* near Ledbury with a railtour on 14 June 1975. Surprisingly, none of the 'Granges' found their way to Dai Woodham's South Wales premises, with the result that it is currently a type unrepresented in preservation. However, at the time of writing, plans are in hand for the construction of one of these engines, which may include components reclaimed from other former Barry survivors that are in course of rebuilding or not yet renovated. This will be identified as No 6880 *Betton Grange*.
D. B. Clark

Postscript: In 1901, during William Dean's tenure, plans were drawn up by Churchward for a basic range of six standard classes, including a mixed-traffic 4-6-0 with 5ft 8in wheels. However, this idea was not taken forward when Churchward assumed the reigns in 1902. He later decided that a mixed-traffic 2-8-0 with this wheel diameter would be useful, and No 4700 appeared in 1919, initially with the Standard No 1 boiler. This was later replaced with the larger No 7 boiler used solely on the nine examples built. It was, therefore, left to Collett to introduce his 'Grange' design, first envisaged in the Dean era. No 4704 poses at Old Oak Common on 27 October 1957. *R. C. Riley*

Index of Locations

Front cover: No 7823 *Hook Norton Manor* heads the 'Cambrian Coast Express' alongside the River Severn near Moat Lane Junction on 8 August 1962. *J. G. Dewing*

Back cover: No 6868 *Penrhos Grange* is illustrated in charge of the 10.05am Exeter to Paignton near Teignmouth on 14 July 1958. *R. C.Riley*

Full details of Ian Allan Publishing titles can be found on
www.ianallanpublishing.com
or by writing for a free copy of our latest catalogue to:
Marketing Dept., Ian Allan Publishing, Riverdene Business Park, Molesey Road, Hersham KT12 4RG.

For an unrivalled range of aviation, military, transport and maritime publications, visit our secure on-line bookshop at
www.ianallansuperstore.com

or visit the Ian Allan Bookshops in
Birmingham
47 Stephenson Street, B2 4DH;
Tel: 0121 643 2496; *e-mail:* ia-birmingham@btconnect.com
Cardiff
31 Royal Arcade, CF10 1AE;
Tel: 02920 390615; *e-mail:* ianallancar@btconnect.com
London
45/46 Lower Marsh, Waterloo, SE1 7RG;
Tel: 020 7401 2100; *e-mail:* ia-waterloo@btconnect.com
Manchester
5 Piccadilly Station Approach, M1 2GH; Tel: 0161 237 9840;
e-mail: ia-manchester@btconnect.com
and (aviation and military titles only) at the
Aviation Experience, Birmingham International Airport
3rd Floor, Main Terminal, B26 3QJ;
Tel: 0121 781 0921; *e-mail:* ia-bia@btconnect.com

or through mail order by writing to:
Ian Allan Mail Order Dept.,
4 Watling Drive, Hinckley LE10 3EY.
Tel: 01455 254450.
Fax: 01455 233737.
e-mail: midlandbooks@compuserve.com

You are only a visit away from over 1,000 publishers worldwide.